A MODERN APPROACH TO

Part Two

CLASSICAL GUITAR
Repertoire

A Graded Anthology of Solo Pieces
(Intermediate to difficult)

By
CHARLES DUNCAN

Supplement to Book Three (and Beyond) of
A Modern Approach to Classical Guitar

HAL•LEONARD®
CORPORATION
7777 W. BLUEMOUND RD. P.O. BOX 13819 MILWAUKEE, WI 53213

CONTENTS

FOREWORD

A Modern Approach to Classical Guitar Repertoire represents a graded anthology of some of the most attractive music from the standard repertoire of 16th through 19th century pieces. The music is carefully arranged in sequence according to the level of difficulty. Part One progresses from easy to intermediate level pieces; Part Two from intermediate through difficult.

The entry achievement level for this book correlates approximately with the mid-point of Book Three of **A Modern Approach to Classical Guitar Playing**. The difficulty of the pieces progresses gradually to a high level of instrumental challenge. Several masterworks of the guitar are included toward the end of the book. Included also are some pieces which will be comparatively unfamiliar, together with many intermediate classical "standards" presented here with a fresh approach to fingering and interpretation. This approach to repertoire should make the book attractive and useful to accomplished students, as well as those who are entering an intermediate level of study.

ALPHABETICAL LIST OF COMPOSERS

PAVANA IN C

Luis Milan

Maestoso M.M. ♩ = 92

*Use a hinge-bar here; i.e., keep the tip of the 1st finger down while raising the
upper part of the finger to play the open string; clamp down again for the C.

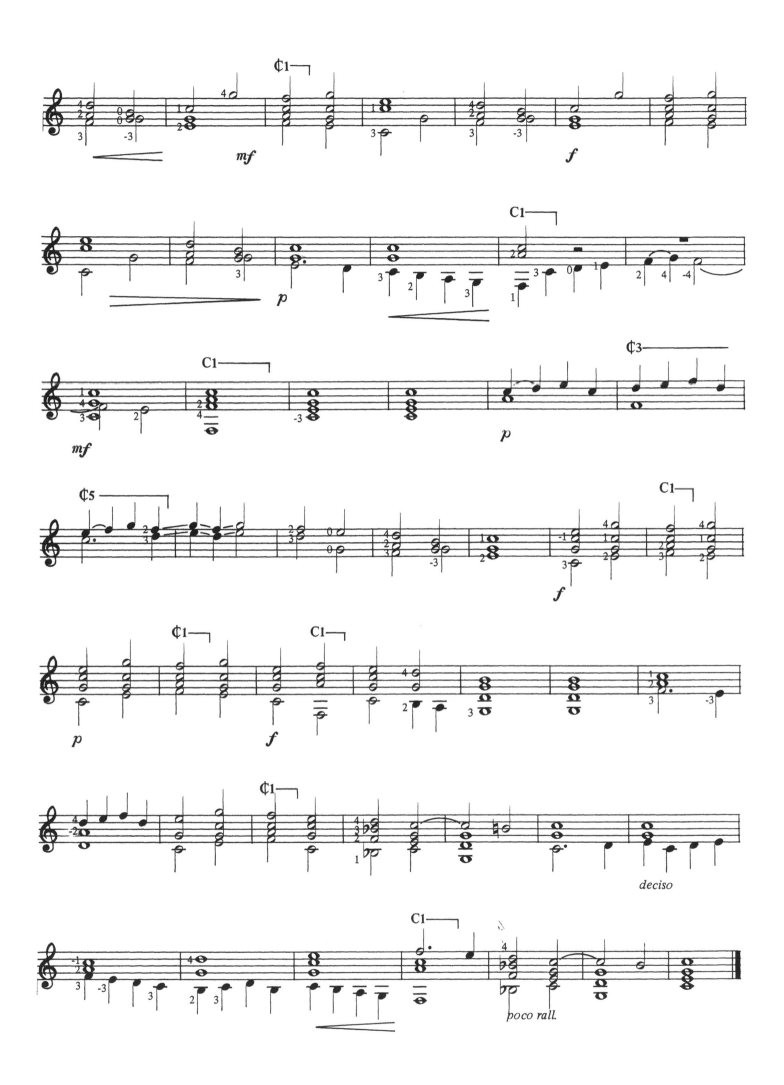

ETUDE IN E MINOR

Fernando Sor

Adagio M.M. ♩ = 72

SALTARELLO

Anon. 16th c.

BALLETTO

Anon. 16th c.

GAGLIARDA

Anon. 16th c.

LA VOLTA

Vivace M.M. ♩ = 184

Anon. 16th c.

WALTZ

Allegro M.M. ♩ = 138

Matteo Carcassi

SARABANDE

Robert de Visée

ETUDE IN A MINOR

Matteo Carcassi

Allegretto M.M. ♩ = 92+

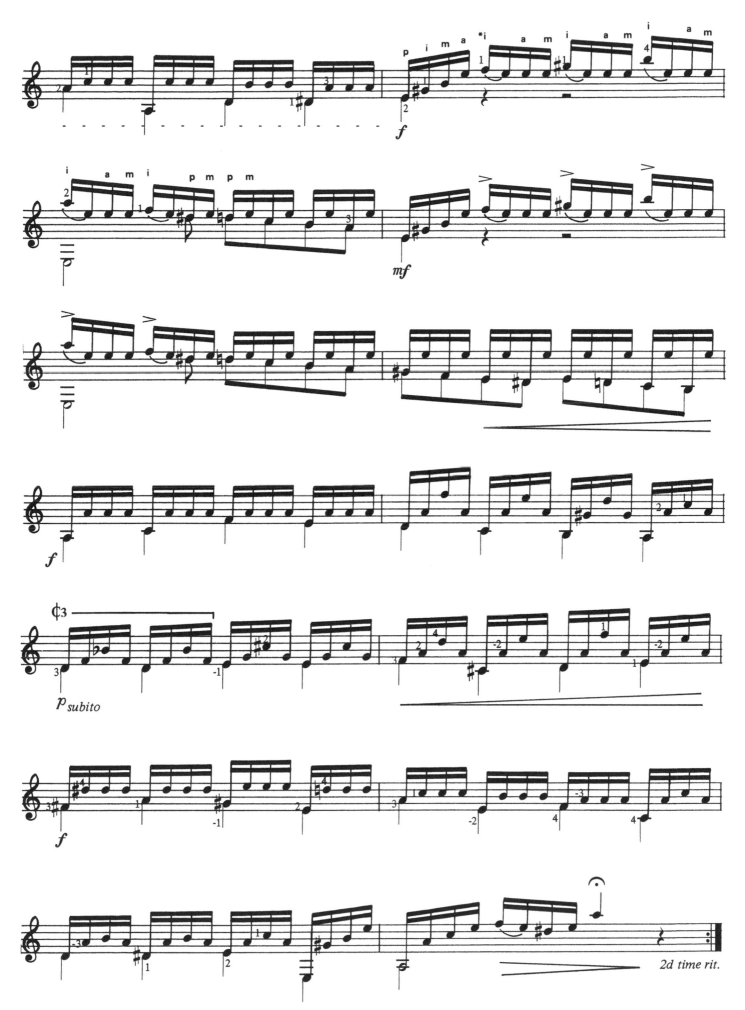

*Use a rest - stroke with **i**, free-stroke with **a** and **m**.

FANFARE

Jean Mouret
Arranged by Charles Duncan

Allegro Moderato M.M. ♩ = 132

MINUET

Anton Diabelli

REVERIE

Charles Duncan

Espressivo M.M. ♩ = 108

*Note key signature — in the key of B♭, both B and E are flatted. Although little classical guitar music is written in the flat keys because of the lack of open strings, these keys are widely used in other forms of music. The piece above, despite the somewhat unfamiliar key signature, is very melodic and not hard to play.

BOURÉE

Count Bergen

19

MEDITATION

Fernando Sor

Affetuoso M.M. ♩ = 104

*Hinge — bar.

WALTZ

Fernando Sor

*Slide — slur.
**Use the flattened 3rd or 4th finger to play these harmonics.

ETUDE IN A

Matteo Carcassi

*Use rest-stroke with **a** to accent the melody (up-stem notes).

MINUET IN G

J.S. Bach

Allegretto M.M. ♩ = 120

MARCH

J.S. Bach

Animato M.M. ♩ = 116

*Adjacent-string slur; play the D with **p** and hammer the C♯ from the open 5th string.

MINUET IN C

Fernando Sor

ALMAN

Robert Johnson

Andante con moto M.M. ♩ = 116

*The A sustains through the shift because of instrumental resonance, particularly
by picking up a sympathetic harmonic from the fourth and fifth strings.

ALMAN

John Dowland

*Note the cross-over fingering.

PAVANA IN D

Luis Milan

LÁGRIMA

Francisco Tarrega

Adagio M.M. ♩ = 76-84

PRELUDE

Robert de Visée

Largo M.M. ♩ = 48

SARABANDE

Robert de Visée

Grave M.M. ♩ = 60

ALLEMANDE

Robert de Visée

BOURÉE

Robert de Visée

PRELUDE

J.S. Bach

Agitato M.M. ♩ = 84

marcato il basso

cresc. poco a poco

*Bar with the tip and mid-joint of the 4th finger.

ETUDE IN E MINOR

Mauro Giuliani

Allegro M.M. ♩ = 88

ANDANTINO SOSTENUTO

Mauro Giuliani

PRELUDIO

Gaspar Sanz

Lento M.M. ♩ = 88

PAVANAS

Gaspar Sanz

Maestoso M.M. ♩ = 92

ESPAÑOLETA

Gaspar Sanz

CANARIOS

Gaspar Sanz

QUEEN ELIZABETH'S GALLIARD

John Dowland

PRELUDE

Francisco Tarrega

Andante sostenuto M.M. ♪ = 96

RH arm. XII

MELODIA ESPAÑOLA

Attributed to Luis Romero
Arranged by Charles Duncan

Andante M.M. ♩ = 92

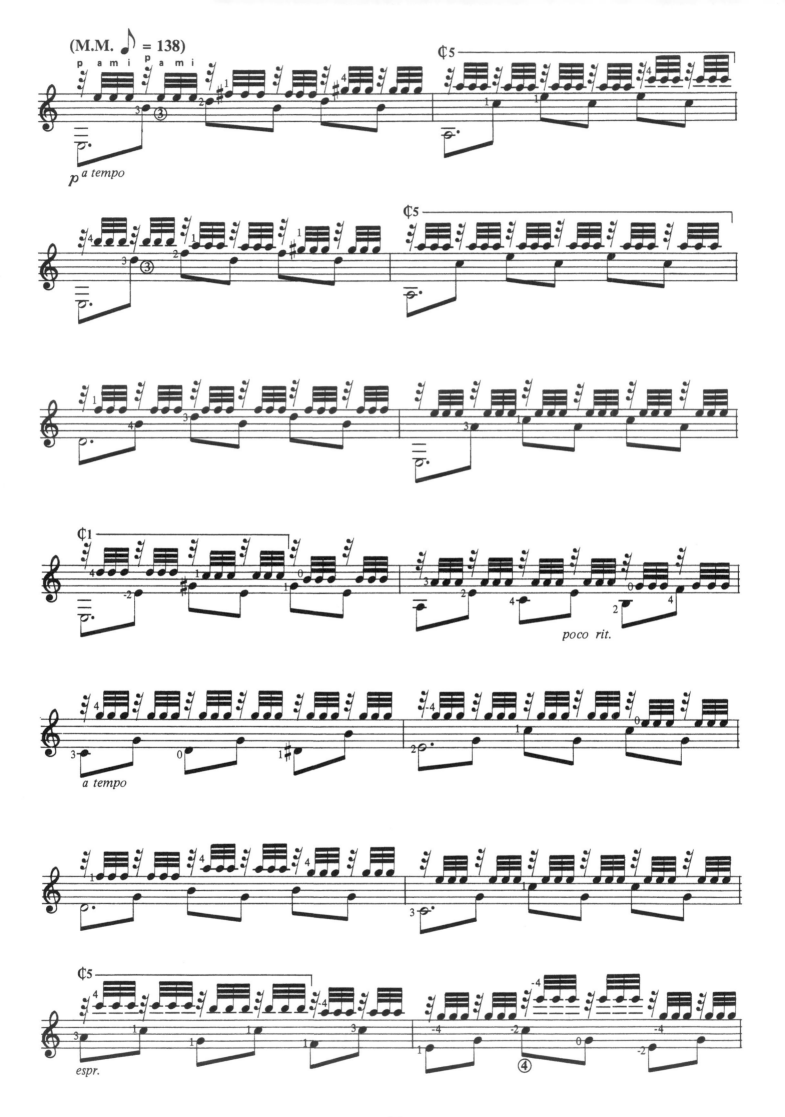

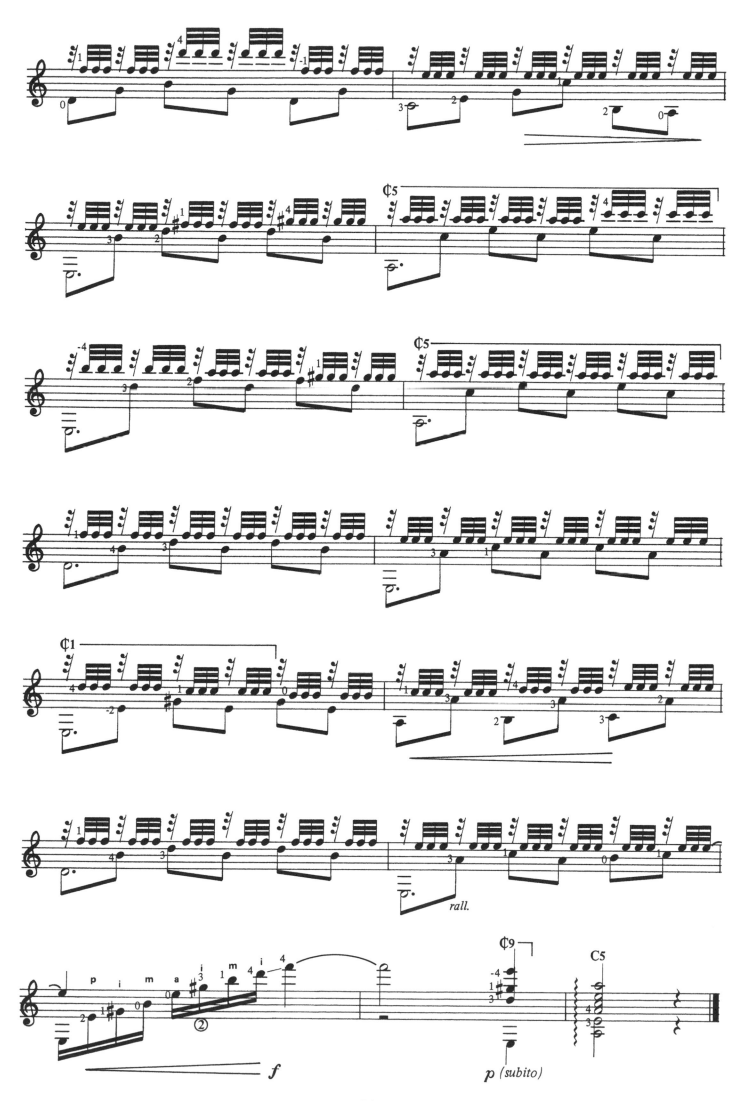

PRELUDE AND ALLEGRO

Santiago de Murcia

(Allegro M.M. ♩ = 184)

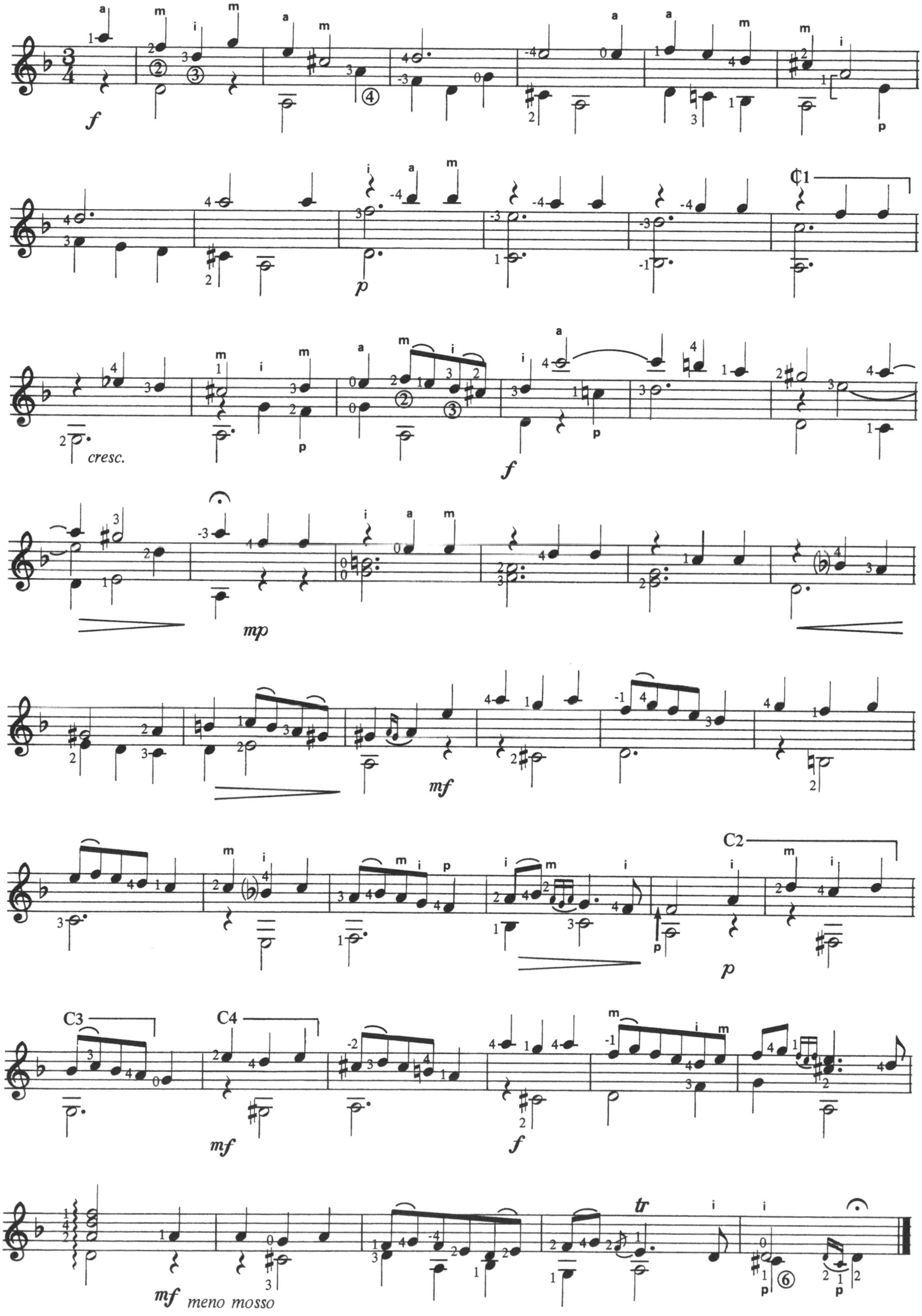

DIFERENCIAS SOBRE
GUARDAME LAS VACAS

Luis de Narvaez

*Optional repeat for each double-bar section up to the Coda.

FANTASÍA

Alonso Mudarra

*Note the crossover fingering for this chord, here and later on in the piece.

*Bring out the syncopation by accenting here.

SONATA IN A

Domenico Scarlatti

Allegro M.M. ♩ = 88

APPALACHIAN ETUDE

Edward Hamler

*Use a rest-stroke with **a** on melody notes.

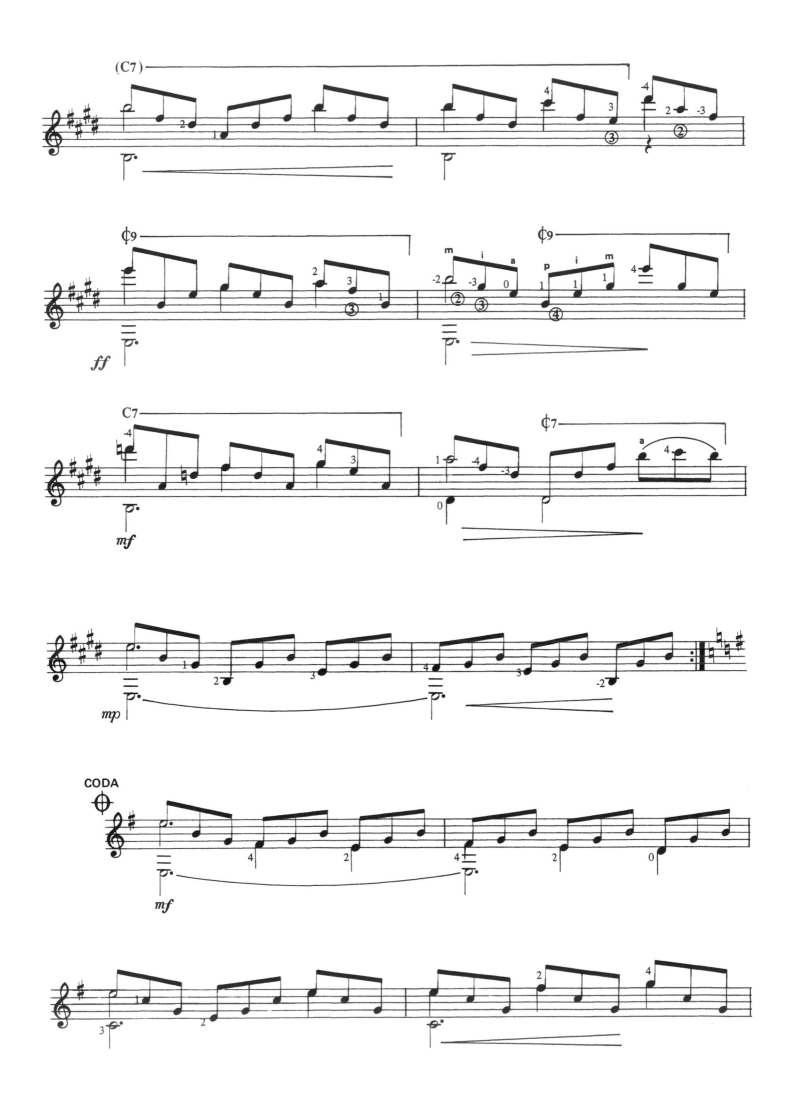

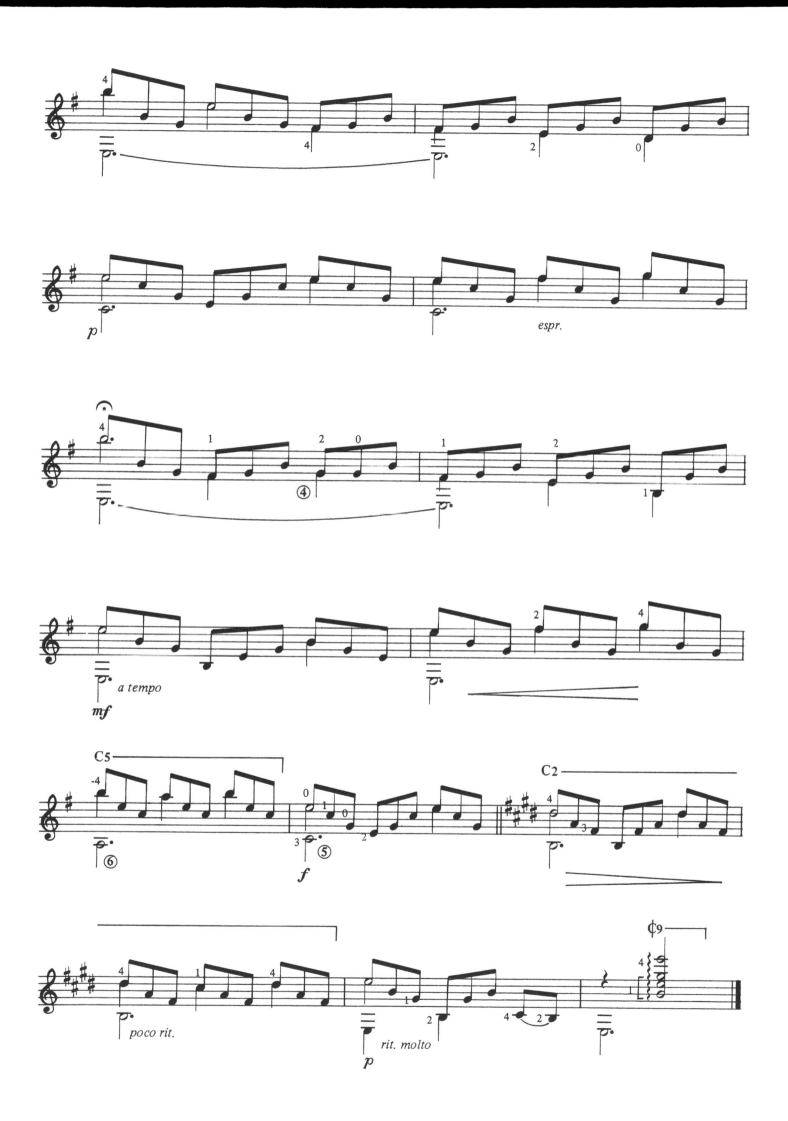

ASTURIAS

Isaac Albéniz

*Both the 6th and 5th string E's are to be played simultaneously, on the beat. Use
a quick down-stroke of the thumb, bringing it to rest against the fourth string.

67

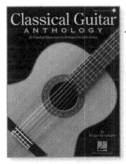

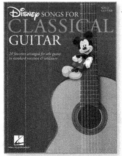